My First Words
A - Z
English to German

Bilingual Learning Made Fun and Easy with Words and Pictures

by Sharon Purtill

Books

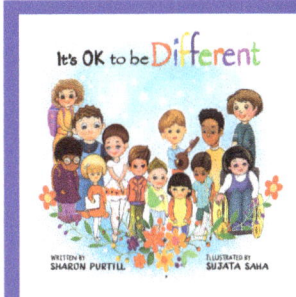 

Bücher

Meine ersten Worte
Englisch zu Deutsch

When learning German it is important to use the article (masculine, feminine or neutral) in front of any noun. These articles are der, die and das.

My First Words A-Z
English to German

Bilingual Learning Made Fun and
Easy with Words and Pictures

by Sharon Purtill

Published by Dunhill Clare Publishing - Ontario, Canada
Copyright 2021 Dunhill Clare Publishing
dunhillclare@gmail.com

Edited by Christine Oana Schüller

Revised October 2023

All rights reserved. No part of this publication may be reproduced, stored in a retrieval system or transmitted, in any form or by any means, electronic, mechanical, photocopying, recording or otherwise without the prior permission of the copyright holder except when embodied in a brief review or mention.

Paperback edition ISBN: 978-1-989733-78-3
Digital edition   ISBN: 978-1-989733-79-0

Library and Archives Canada Cataloguing in Publications

Apple

der Apfel

Books

die Bücher

Cat

die Katze

Dog

der Hund

Elephant

der Elefant

Flower

die Blume

Giraffe

die Giraffe

Hat

der Hut

Ice Cream

das Eis

Jacket

die Jacke

Keys

die Schlüssel

Leaf

das Blatt

Milk

die Milch

Nest

das Nest

Orange

die Orange

Pail

der Eimer

Quilt

die Decke

Rabbit

der Hase

Shoe

der Schuh

Table

der Tisch

Umbrella

der Regenschirm

Vacuum

der Staubsauger

Watermelon

die Wassermelone

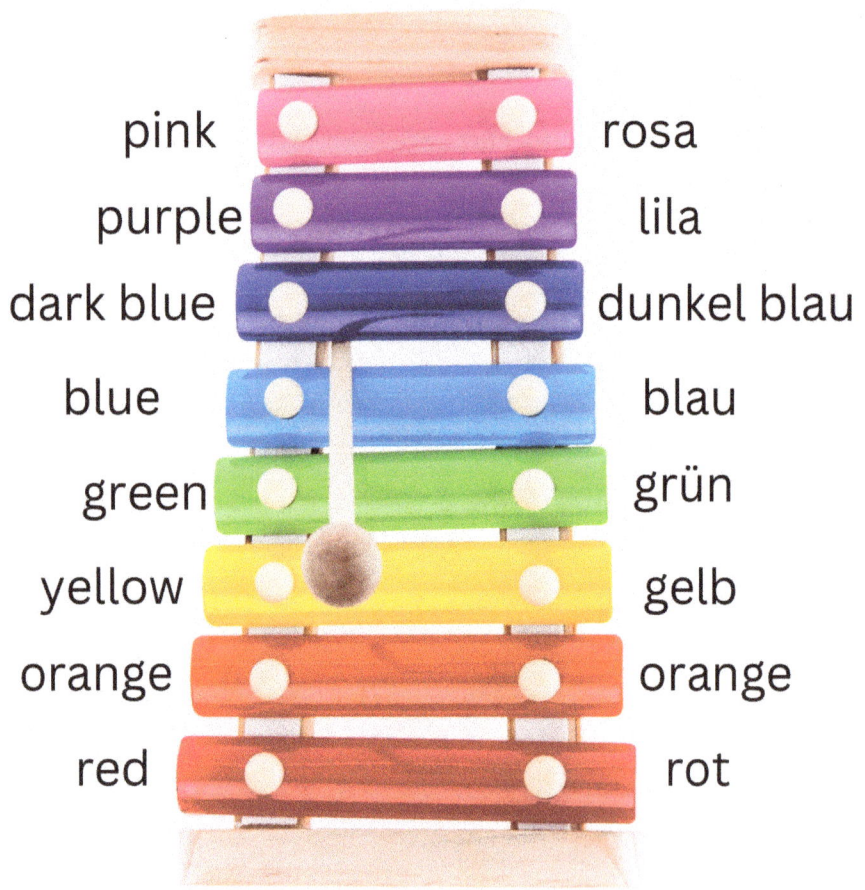

yellow

gelb

Zebra

das Zebra

Bonus Words

English and German

Let's learn common words for things found in and around the home.

oh what
FUN

Found in the Kitchen
In der Küche gefunden

Plate		der Teller
Fork		die Gabel
Spoon		der Löffel
Knife		das Messer
Bowl		die Schüssel
Cup		die Tasse

Found in the Bathroom
Gefunden im Badezimmer

Toothpaste		die Zahnpasta
Toothbrush		die Zahnbürste
Brush		die Bürste
Comb		der Kamm
Towel		das Handtuch

Found in the Bedroom
Gefunden im Schlafzimmer

Bed  das Bett

Blankets  die Decken

Pillow  das Kissen

Dresser  die Kommode

Toys  die Spielzeuge

Found in the Living Room
Gefunden im Wohnzimmer

Television — der Fernseher

Chair — der Stuhl

Rug — der Teppich

Lamp — die Lampe

Sofa — das Sofa

Found Outside
Draußen gefunden

Tree  der Baum

Car  das Auto

Truck  der Lastwagen

Bike  das Fahrrad

Grass  das Gras

www.ingramcontent.com/pod-product-compliance
Lightning Source LLC
Chambersburg PA
CBHW050740080526
44579CB00017B/111